THE 2000s

T0204812

**MELODY LINE, CHORDS AND LYRICS
FOR KEYBOARD • GUITAR • VOCAL**

HAL•LEONARD®

ISBN 978-1-4234-5966-8

HAL•LEONARD®
CORPORATION
7777 W. BLUEMOUND RD. P.O. BOX 13819 MILWAUKEE, WI 53213

Visit Hal Leonard Online at
www.halleonard.com

Welcome to the PAPERBACK SONGS SERIES.

Do you play piano, guitar, electronic keyboard, sing or play any instrument for that matter? If so, this handy "pocket tune" book is for you.

The concise, one-line music notation consists of:

MELODY, LYRICS & CHORD SYMBOLS

Whether strumming the chords on guitar, "faking" an arrangement on piano/keyboard or singing the lyrics, these fake book style arrangements can be enjoyed at any experience level – hobbyist to professional.

The musical skills necessary to successfully use this book are minimal. If you play guitar and need some help with chords, a basic chord chart is included at the back of the book.

While playing and singing is the first thing that comes to mind when using this book, it can also serve as a compact, comprehensive reference guide.

However you choose to use this PAPERBACK SONGS SERIES book, by all means, have fun!

CONTENTS

APOLOGIZE

Words and Music by
RYAN TEDDER

I said it's too late to 'pol - o - gize.

It's too late, hey, __ hey, hey. __

Hey, __ hey, I'd

take an - oth - er chance, __ take a fall. Take a shot for you. __

I need you like a heart needs a

beat, but it's noth - in' new, _____ yeah, __ yeah. __ I

loved you with a fire __ red, now it's turn - in'

blue, _____ and you say _____

sor - ry like an an - gel heav-en let me think was you. _

_ But, I'm _ a - fraid _ it's too late to'pol - o - gize. _

_ It's too late. _____ I said it's

too late to'pol - o - gize. _____ It's too late, _____

_ whoa, _ whoa. _____ Hey,

_ hey, hey. _ Hey, _

BAD DAY

Words and Music by
DANIEL POWTER

Where is the mo - ment we need - ed the most? __

You kick up the leaves __ and the mag - ic is lost. __

They tell me your blue __ skies fade __ to grey. __

__ They tell me your pas - sion's gone __ a - way __

__ and I don't need __ no car - ryin'on. __

You stand in the line __ just to hit a new low. __

You're fak-in' the smile __ with the cof-fee to go. __

__ They tell me your life's __ been way __ off line. __

__ You've fall-en to piec - es ev - 'ry time __

__ and I don't need __ no car - ryin' on __

__ be - cause you had a bad

day. You're tak-in' one down. You sing a sad

song just to turn it a - round. __ You say you don't

know. You tell me don't lie. You work at a smile _

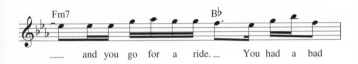

_ and you go for a ride. _ You had a bad

day. The cam - 'ra don't lie. You're com - in' back

down and you real - ly don't mind. You had a bad

day. ___ You had a bad day. *Instrumental*

Well, you need a blue _ sky hol - i - day. _

The point is they laugh __ at what __ you say __

__ and I don't need __ no car - ryin' on. _____ You had a bad

day. __ Oh, _____ on a hol - i - day. ____

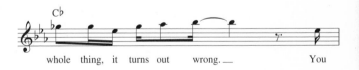

Some-times the sys - tem goes __ on the blink __ and the

whole thing, it turns out wrong. __ You

might not make it back __ and you know __ that you could

be well. Oh, that's strong __ and I'm not wrong, __

yeah.

So where is the pas - sion when you need it the most?

Oh, ____ you and I. ____

____ You kick up the leaves ____ and the mag - ic is lost ____

____ 'cause you had a bad

day. You're tak - in' one down. You sing a sad

song just to turn it a - round. You say you don't

know. You tell me don't lie. You work at a smile

and you go for a ride. You had a bad

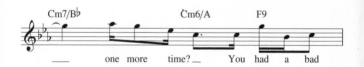

day. You've seen what you like. And how does it feel

one more time? You had a bad

day. You had a bad day. *(Vocal ad lib.)*

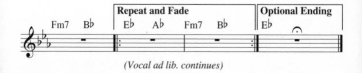

(Vocal ad lib. continues)

BEAUTIFUL

Words and Music by
LINDA PERRY

Cm   **A♭**

I am beau - ti - ful _____ in
You are beau - ti - ful _____ in
We are beau - ti - ful _____ in

Fm   **E♭**   **E♭/D♭**

ev -'ry sin - gle way. _ Yes, words can't bring me _ down, _
ev -'ry sin - gle way. _ Yes, words can't bring you _ down, _
ev -'ry sin - gle way. _ Yes, words won't bring us _ down, _

Cm   **1, 3**   **Fm7**   **To Coda ⊕**

_____ oh _ no. _____ So don't you bring me down _
_____ oh _ no. _____
_____ oh _ no. _____ So don't you bring me down _

E♭   **E♭/D♭**   **Cm**   **B(♭5)**

to - day. _

2   **Fm7**

So don't you _ bring me down to - day. _

E♭   **E♭/D♭**

_____ No mat ter what _ we do. _ No mat ter what _ we say. _

BEAUTIFUL SOUL

Words and Music by ANDY DODD
and ADAM WATTS

one I want to hold. ___ I won't let an - oth - er

min - ute go ___ to waste. ___ I want

To Coda ⊕

you and your ___ beau-ti - ful soul. ___

Your beau - ti-ful soul, ___ yeah. ___

___ You might ___ need time ___

you and your ___ beau-ti - ful soul. ___

Am I   cra-zy   for want-in'   you? _

Ba - by,   do   you think   you could want   me   too? __

I don't wan-na   waste _ your time. _____   Do you

see things the way I   do? _   I just want to know that you feel it too. __

There   is   noth - ing   left   to   hide. __

I don't want an - oth - er

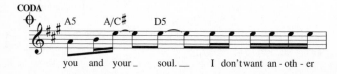

you   and your _   soul. __   I don't want an - oth - er

(Vocal ad lib.)

BEST OF YOU

Words and Music by DAVE GROHL, TAYLOR HAWKINS,
CHRIS SHIFLETT and NATE MENDEL

Moderately fast

I've got an-oth-er con-fes - sion to make: _

I'm _ your fool. _

Ev - 'ry-one's got their chains _ to break _

hold - ing you. _

Were you born to re - sist, _____

_____ or be _ a - bused? _____

Is some-one get-ting the best, _____ the best, _____ the best, _

_____ the best _ of you? _

Is some-one get-ting the best, _____ the best, _____ the best, _

_____ the best _ of you? _

Are you gone _ and on _____ to some - one new? _

_____ I need-ed some-where to hang _

_ my head _____ with - out _ your noose. _
_ a - gain, _____ but I _____ break loose. _

You gave me some-thing that I ___
My head is giv - ing me life ___

___ did-n't have, ___ but had ___ no use. ___
___ or death, ___ but I ___ can't choose. ___

I was too weak to give in, ___
I swear I'll nev - er give in, ___

too strong ___ to lose. ___
I ___ re - fuse. ___

My heart is un - der ar - rest ___ ___

Is some-one get-ting the best, ___ the best, ___ the best, ___

___ the best ___ of you? ___

F#7(add4)　　　　　　　　　　　C#m7

Is some-one get-ting the best, __ the best, _ the best, _

Bsus　　　　　　　　　　　　Asus2

__ the best __ of you? __

F#7(add4)　　　　　　　　　　　C#m7

Has some-one tak-en your faith? _ It's real, __ the pain _

Bsus　　　　　　　　　　　　Asus2

__ you feel. _ Your trust, __ you must _ con - fess. _

F#7(add4)　　　　　　　　　　　C#m7

__ Is some-one get-ting the best, __ the best, _ the best, _

Bsus　　　　　　　　　　　　Asus2

__ the best __ of you? __

F#7(add4)　　　　　　　　　　　C#m7

Oh. __　　　　　　　　　　　　*Instrumental*

Asus2　　　　　　　　　　　　C#m7

Oh, _____ oh, _____

_____ oh, _____

oh. Has some - one tak - en your faith? _

Half-time feel

_____ It's real, _ the pain _ you feel. _ The life, _

_____ the love you thought _____ you healed. _ The hope _

_____ that stops _ the bro - ken hearts. _ Your trust, _

the best of you?

Has some-one tak-en your faith? It's real, the pain

you feel. Your trust, you must con-fess.

Is some-one get-ting the best, the best, the best,

the best of you?

Oh.

Instrumental

BLEEDING LOVE

Words and Music by JESSE McCARTNEY and RYAN TEDDER

Moderately

Closed off from love, I did-n't need the pain.

Once or twice was e-nough and it was all in vain.

Time starts to pass; be-fore you know it you're fro-

-zen, oh.

But some-thin' hap-pened for the ver-y first time with you.

My heart melts in-to the ground, found some-thing true.

And ev-'ry-one's look-ing 'round think-in' I'm go-in' cra-

-zy, hey. _____

But I don't care what they say, __ I'm in love _ with you. _

__ They try to pull me a-way, __ but they don't know _ the truth. _

__ My heart's crip-pled by the vein that I keep on clos-

- in'. You cut me o-pen and I __

__ keep bleed-in', keep, __ keep bleed-in' love. _

Dm7

____ I keep bleed-in', I keep, ____ keep bleed-in' love. __

B♭maj7

____ Keep bleed-in', keep, ____ keep bleed-in' love. __

C   **To Coda** ⊕

____   You cut me o - pen.

F

Try-in' hard not to

Dm7

hear, but they talk so loud. __ Their pierc-in' sounds fill my

B♭maj7

ears, try to fill me with doubt. __ Yet, I know that the

Csus

goal is to keep me from fall - ing, hey, __

_____ umm. But noth-in's great-er than the

rush that comes from your em - brace. _ And in this world of lone-

- li-ness, I see _ your face. _____ Yet, ev-'ry-one a - round _

___ me thinks that I'm go - in' cra - zy, may-

- be, may - be.

D.S. al Coda

CODA

You cut me o - pen. _____

And it's drain - in' all _____ of _

___ me. Oh, they find it hard _ to be - lieve. _

BOSTON

Words and Music by DANIEL LAYUS,
JARED PALOMAR, JOSIAH ROZENCWAJG,
and JUSTIN SOUTH

BREAKAWAY

Words and Music by BRIDGET BENENATE,
AVRIL LAVIGNE and MATTHEW GERRARD

44

do what it takes __ 'til I touch the sky. I'll __

make a wish. Take a chance. Make a change and

break - a - way. Out of the dark - ness and

in - to the sun. _____ But I won't for - get __ all the ones __

__ that I love. { I'll __ / I got - ta } take a risk. Take a chance.

To Coda ⊕

Make a change and break - a - way.

Dah, dah, dah, dah, dah. Dah, dah, dah, dah, dah.

46

D.S. al Coda

Am   G   Fsus2

Dah, dah, dah, dah, dah, dah, dah.

CODA

Am   G   Fsus2

break - a - way. _____

G5   C5   F5

Build-ing with a hun-dred floors. Swing-ing 'round re-volv-ing doors.

G5   C5   F5

May-be I don't know where they'll take ____ me. But,

G5   C5   F5

got-ta keep mov-in' on, mov-in' on. Fly a-

D5   F5   G5   C

way, break a - way. _____ I'll spread my wings and I'll

G   Am

learn how to fly. __ Though it's not eas-y to tell __

BREATHE

Words and Music by HOLLY LAMAR
and STEPHANIE BENTLEY

Moderately fast

I can feel the mag - ic float - ing in

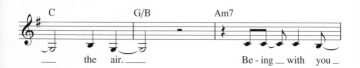

the air. Be - ing with you

gets me that way. I watch the sun -

- light dance a - cross your face and I

nev-er been this swept a - way.

BUBBLY

Words and Music by COLBIE CAILLAT
and JASON REEVES

Please stay for a while ___ now. Just take your time ___

___ wher - ev - er you go. ___

The rain is fall - in' on my win - dow pane,

but we are hid - in' in a saf - er place.

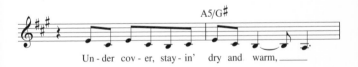

Un - der cov - er, stay - in' dry and warm, ___

you give me feel - ings that ___ I a - dore. It starts in my toes, ___

___ makes me crin - kle my nose. ___ Wher - ev - er it goes, ___

D(add9)   A

_____ I al - ways ___ know ___ that you make me smile. __

A5/G#

____ Please stay for a while ___ now. Just take your time __

D(add9)   **To Coda** ⊕ A   Amaj7/C#

_____ wher-ev - er you go. ___   But

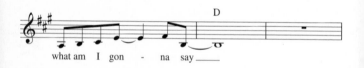

D

what am I gon - na say _____

E(add4)

when you make me feel ___ this

Bm7   Amaj7/C#

way? _____   I ____ just... __

D.S. al Coda

___ Mm.___ And it starts in my toes, __

CODA

Instrumental

I've been a - sleep for a

while _ now. You tucked me in just like a

child _ now. 'Cause ev - 'ry time you hold me

in your arms, ___ I'm com - fort' - ble e - nough to

feel your warmth. It starts in my soul ___ and I lose all con - trol. ___

A5/G#   D(add9)

___ When you kiss my nose, ___ the feel - in' shows ___

A

___ 'cause you make me smile. ___ Ba - by, just take your time ___

A5/G#   D(add9)

___ now, hold - in' me tight. _____

A   **Slower**

___ Wher - ev - er, _____ wher -

Amaj7/G#   D6

ev - er, _____ wher - ev - er ___ you go. ___

Wher - ev – er, _____ wher -

ev - er, ___ wher - ev - er ___ you go. _

Ooh, wher - ev -

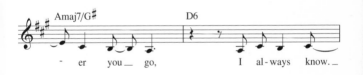

- er you ___ go, I al - ways know. _

_____ 'Cause you make me smile, _

_____ e - ven just for a while. ___

CLOCKS

Words and Music by GUY BERRYMAN, JON BUCKLAND,
WILL CHAMPION and CHRIS MARTIN

Moderately

Lights go out and I can't be saved. _
Con - fu - sion _ nev - er stops. _

Tides that I tried to swim a - gainst _
Clos - ing _ walls and tick - ing clocks _ gon - na

brought me down up - on my knees. _
come back and take you home. _ I

Oh I beg, I beg and plead. _ Sing - in', come out of
could not stop that you now know. _ Sing - in', come out up -

things un - said. _ Shoot an ap - ple off my head. _ And a
on my seas, _ curse missed op - por - tu - ni - ties. _ Am I

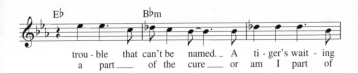

trou - ble that can't be named. _ A ti - ger's wait - ing
a part _ of the cure _ or am I part of

to be tamed. _ } Sing - in', _____ you _
the dis - ease? _ }

are. _

You _____

are. _ *Instrumental*

You __

are. __

You _____ are. __

Instrumental

You _____ are. __

And noth - ing else com - pares. _____

Home, home, ___ where I want - ed ___ to go. Home, home, where I want - ed ___ to go.

Instrumental

Repeat and Fade | **Optional Ending**

COMPLICATED

Words and Music by AVRIL LAVIGNE, LAUREN CHRISTY,
SCOTT SPOCK and GRAHAM EDWARDS

Moderate Pop

F

Chill out, what cha yell - in' for?
You came o - ver un - an - nounced,

Dm

Lay back, it's all been done __ be - fore.
dressed up like you're some - thing else.

Bb(add9)

And if you could on - ly ____
Where you are ain't where __ it's ____

C

let it be ____ you will see. _____
at, you see. ____ You're mak - in' me _____

F

I like you the way __ you are
laugh out when you strike __ your pose.

Dm

when we're driv - in' in _____ your car
Take off all your prep - py clothes.
Lay back, it's all been done _____ be - fore.

B♭(add9)

and you're talk - in' to _____ me
You know you're not fool - in'
And if you could on - ly

C

one on one _____ but you be - come _____
an - y - one _____ when you be - come _____
let it be _____ you will see _____

B♭(add9)

some - bod - y else 'round ev - 'ry - one else. You're

Dm   **To Coda ⊕**

watch - ing your back like you can't re - lax. _____ You're

B♭(add9)

try'n' to be cool. You look like a fool to me. _

64

C5

_____ Tell _____ me,

D5   Bb5

why'd you have to go and make things so com - pli - cat -

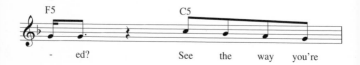

F5   C5

- ed?   See   the   way   you're

D5   Bb5

act - ing like you're some-bod - y else, __ gets me frus - trat -

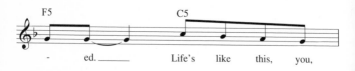

F5   C5

- ed. _____ Life's like this, you,

D5   Bb5

you fall __ and you crawl __ and you break __ and you take __

F5   C5

___ what you get __ and you turn __ it in - to

hon - es - ty and prom-ise me I'm nev - er gon - na find you fake

it, no, no, no. no, no, no, no,

no, no, no, no, no, no, no, no, no, no, no,

D.S. al Coda

no. Chill out, what cha yell - in' for?

CODA

try'n' to be cool. You look like a fool to me.

Tell me

why'd you have to go and make things so com - pli - cat -

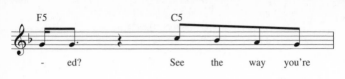

- ed? See the way you're

act - ing like you're some-bod - y else, _ gets me frus - trat -

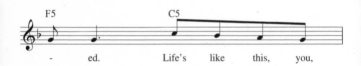

- ed. Life's like this, you,

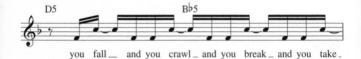

you fall _ and you crawl _ and you break _ and you take _

___ what you get _ and you turn _ it in - to

hon - es - ty. Prom ise me I'm nev - er gon - na find you fake _

_ it, _ no, no, _ it, _ no, no, _ no.

CRAZY

Words and Music by BRIAN BURTON,
THOMAS CALLAWAY, GIANPIERO REVERBERI
and GIANFRANCO REVERBERI

Moderate R&B

I re-mem-ber when, I re-

mem-ber, I re-mem-ber when I lost my mind. __ There was

some-thing so pleas-ant a-bout __ that place. __

__ E-ven your e-mo-tions have an ech-o in so much space. __

__ Umm, __

- zy?___ Pos - si - bly.___

___ And I hope that you ___ are hav-

- in' ___ the time ___ of ___ your life,___

but think twice.___

That's my on - ly ad - vice, ___ umm. ___

Come on now, who do you, who do

you, who do you, who do you think you are?____

E♭maj7

— Ha, — ha, ha, — bless — your soul._____

A♭(add9)   A♭

—   You real-ly think you're in con-trol? _

Gsus   G   Cm

—   Well, I think you're cra - zy. ____

E♭maj7

I think you're cra - zy. _____

A♭(add9)

I think you're cra - zy _____

just like me. _____

_____ My he - roes had the heart _

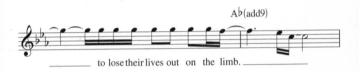

_____ to lose their lives out on the limb. _____

And all I re-mem - ber _____ is think-

- in', I wan-na be like them. __

Umm, _____

_____ ev - er since I was lit - tle, ev - er

since I was lit-tle it looked like fun. ___ And it's

no co-in - ci - dence _ I've come _____

and I can die when I'm done. _____

But, may - be I'm cra - zy. _____

May - be you're cra - zy. _____

May-be we're cra - zy, ____ prob - a - bly. _

Umm, ____

_____ ooh, _____

_ umm, _____ woo, ____

____ umm. _____

CRAZY IN LOVE

Words and Music by RICH HARRISON,
SHAWN CARTER and BEYONCE KNOWLES

Moderate Hip Hop

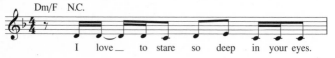

I love _ to stare so deep in your eyes.

I touch _ on you more and more ev - 'ry time.

When you leave, I'm beg - gin' you not to go.

Call your name two or three times in a row.

Such a fun - ny thing for me to try to ex - plain,

how I'm feel - in' and my pride is the one to blame.

Dm/F   N.C.

'Cause I know I don't un - der -stand

just how __ your love can do what no one else can.

Bb

Got me look - in' so cra - zy right now, your love's __

G

__ got me look - in' so cra - zy right now. Your love __

Bb

__ got me look - in' so cra - zy right now. Your touch __

G

__ got me look - in' so cra - zy right now. Your touch __

Bb

__ got me hop - in' you'll page __ me right now. Your kiss __

G

got me hop - in' you'll save __ me right now.

B♭

Look - in' so cra - zy, your love's __ got me look - in', got me

To Coda ⊕

G   Dm/F N.C.

look - in' so crazy in love. __   Uh - oh, uh - oh, uh - oh, oh, no no.

Dm/F N.C.

Uh oh, uh - oh, uh - oh, oh, no no.   Uh oh, uh - oh, uh - oh, oh, no no.

Uh - oh, uh - oh, uh - oh, oh, no - no.

Dm/F N.C.

When I talk to my friends so qui - et - ly,

who he think he is? Look at what you did to me.

Dm/F N.C.

Ten-nis shoes, don't e-ven need to buy a new __ dress.

If you ain't there, ain't no-bod-y else to im - press.

Dm/F N.C.

It's just the way that you know what I thought I knew.

It the beat that my heart skips when I'm with you. _____

Dm/F   N.C.

But I still don't un - der -stand

D.S. al Coda

just how __ your love can do what no one else can.

CODA

Bb

Look-in' so cra - zy, your love's __ got me look-in', got me

look-in' so cra-zy in love. _ Rap: *(See additional lyrics)*

Uh-oh, uh-oh, uh -oh, oh, no-no. Uh oh, uh-oh, uh-oh, oh, no-no.
Rap ends

Got me look - in' _ so cra - zy, _ my ba - by. _ I'm

not my - self _ late ly. I'm fool - ish, _ I don't do this. _ I've been

play-in' my - self. _ Ba-by, I don't _ care. ___'Cause your _ love's _

_ got the best of me. _ And, ba - by, you're mak -

got me hop - in' you'll save — me right now.

Look - in' so cra - zy, your love's got me look - in', got me

look - in' so cra - zy in love. —

1

Got me look - in' so cra - zy right now, your love's—

2

Repeat and Fade

Optional Ending

Additional Lyrics

Rap: Young Hov, y'all know when the flow is loco.
Young B and the R-O-C, uh-oh.
Ol' G, big homey, the one and only.
Stick bony, but the pocket is fat like Tony Soprano.
The ROC handle like Van Axel.
I shake phonies, man, you can't get next to the genuine article,
   I do not sing low.
I sling though, if anything I bling yo'.
A star like Ringo, roar like a gringo.
Bret if you're crazy, bring your whole set.
Jay-Z in the range, crazy and deranged.
They can't figure him out, they like "Hey, is he insane?"
Yes sir, I'm cut from a different cloth.
My texture is the best fur chinchilla.
I been healin' the chain smokers.
How you think I got the name Hova?
I been realer, the game's over.
Fall back young, ever since the label changed over to platinum
   the game's been a wrap, one.

DON'T KNOW WHY

Words and Music by
JESSE HARRIS

Moderately slow

82

DRIFT AWAY

Words and Music by
MENTOR WILLIAMS

Moderately fast

Day af - ter day I'm more con -
Be - gin - ning to think that I'm wast - in'
And thanks for the joy that you've giv - en

fused;
time;   I look for the
me;   don't un - der-
                                   I want you to

light in the pour - ing rain. _____
stand the things that I do. _____
know I be - lieve in your song, _____

You know __ that's a
'Cause the world out -
and rhythm _ and

game that I hate to lose.
side looks so un - kind.
rhyme and har - mo - ny.

I'm feel - in' the strain;
Now I'm count - in' on you
You help me a - long,

To Coda ⊕

ain't __ it a shame? __ }
to car - ry me through. __ }
mak - in' me strong. __

Oh,

give me the beat, __ boys, to soothe my soul; __ I

wan - na get lost in your rock __ and roll __ and

drift a - way. __

D

Give me the beat, boys, to soothe my soul; I

A

wan-na get lost in your rock and roll and

G

drift a - way.

1					2
D	A	G/B	A	D	N.C.

Instrumental

Em

And when my

mind is free no mel - o - dy can

D   **Em**

move me.   When I'm

feel - in' blue ___   gui - tars   are

com - in' through ___   to   soothe ___ me.

D.C. al Coda   **CODA**

Give me the beat, ___ boys, to soothe my soul;   I

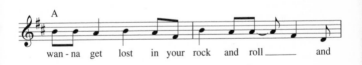

wan - na get lost in your rock and roll ___ and

drift a - way. ___

Repeat and Fade   **Optional Ending**

DRIVE

Words and Music by BRANDON BOYD,
MICHAEL EINZIGER, ALEX KATUNICH,
JOSE PASILLAS II and CHRIS KILMORE

Moderate Rock

Some-times, I feel the fear of the un-

cer-tain-ty sting-ing clear.

And I can't help but ask myself how much I'll

let the fear take the wheel and steer.

It's driv-en me be-fore and it seems to have a vague

haunt - ing mass ap-peal.

90

be one of ___ the hive, ___

will I ___ choose wa-ter o - ver wine ___ and hold my

own and drive, ___ ah, ___ ah, ah, ah, ___ oh? ___

It's driv-en me be - fore ___ and it seems ___ to be ___ the way ___

_____ that ev-'ry-one ___ else gets ___ a - round. ___

___ Late-ly I'm ___ be-gin-ning to find ___ that when ___

D.S. al Coda

___ I drive ___ my - self, ___ my light ___ is found.

CODA

Instrumental

Would you choose _____ wa-ter o - ver wine, _

_____ hold _ the _ wheel _ and drive?

What-ev - er to-mor - row brings, _ I'll _ be _

_ there _ with o-pen arms _ and o - pen eyes, _ yeah! _

What-ev - er to - mor - row brings, _ I'll _ be _

_ there, _ I'll be _ there. _____ Do, do, do, _

_ do, do, do, _ do, do, do, _ do, do, bom, bom, _

_ bom, do, do, do, _ do, do. ___ Do, do, do, _

_ do, do, do, _ do, do, do, _ do, do, bom, bom, _

_ bom bom _ bom. _

FALLIN'

Words and Music by
ALICIA KEYS

Freely

N.C.

I keep on fall-in' in ____ *(Vocal ad lib.)* and

Moderate Blues tempo

Em   Bm7   Em   Bm7

out of love   with-a   you.   Some-times __ I

Em   Bm7   Em   Bm7

love you   some-times you make me blue.   Some-times I feel

Em   Bm7   Em   Bm7

good.   At times I feel used.   Lov-ing you

Em   Bm7   Em   Bm7

dar - ling __   makes me so con - fused.   I ____ keep on

Em   Bm7   Em   Bm7

fall - in'   in and out __   of love   with-a you. I _____

94

96

FLYING WITHOUT WINGS

Words and Music by WAYNE HECTOR
and STEVE MAC

Moderate Ballad

Ev-'ry-bod-y's look - ing for that some - thing.

One thing that makes __ it all __ com - plete. __

You'll find it in __ the strang - est plac - es. __

Plac - es you nev - er knew __ it could be.

Some find it in __ the fac - es of their

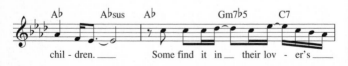

chil - dren. __ Some find it in __ their lov - er's

Db
oth - ers. _____

Cm7   Fm7
A sim-ple line can make you laugh _ or _____

Bbm7   Eb7sus   Eb/G
cry. _____   You'll find it in __ the deep - est

Ab   Absus   Ab   Gm7b5   C7
friend ships.   The kind you cher - ish all __ your __

Fm7 Absus/F Fm7   Eb
life.   And when you know _ how much _ that means _

Db   Eb7sus   Eb7
__ you've found that spe-cial thing. _ You're fly-ing with out

Ab   Absus   Ab   Bbm7 Ab/C Db Db+ Db6 Bb/D
wings.   So im-pos - si - ble   as __ they may

seem, you've got to fight for ev - 'ry

dream. 'Cause who's to know which one you let

go _____ would have made you com -

plete? _____ But for me it's wak - ing up be -

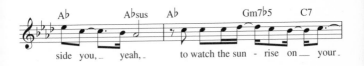

side you, _ yeah, _ to watch the sun - rise on _ your _

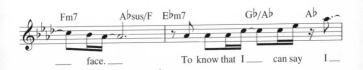

_ face. _ To know that I _ can say I _

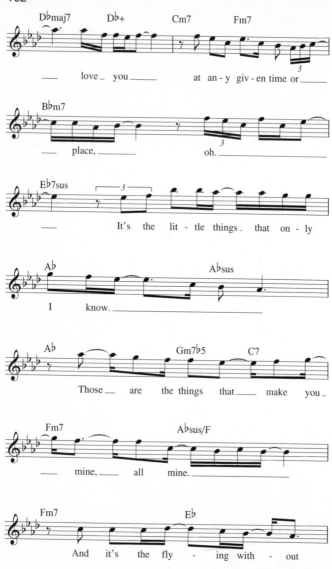

THE GAME OF LOVE

Words and Music by RICK NOWELS
and GREGG ALEXANDER

106

HEAVEN

Words and Music by HENRY GARZA,
JOEY GARZA and RINGO GARZA

Moderately

Save _____ me from this pris - on. ___

Lord, help me get a - way. ___

'Cause on - ly you can save me now ___

___ from this mis - er - y. _____

I've _____ been lost in my own place ___

___ and I'm get - tin' wea - ry. ___ How _ far is

heav - en? _ And I _____ know that I need to change _

* Recorded a half step lower.

HERE WITHOUT YOU

Words and Music by MATT ROBERTS,
BRAD ARNOLD, CHRISTOPHER HENDERSON
and ROBERT HARRELL

*Recorded a half step lower.

I'm here with - out ___ you, ba - by,

but you're still on ___ my lone - ly mind. ___

I think a - bout ___ you, ba - by,

and I dream a - bout ___ you all _____ the time. ___

I'm here with - out ___ you, ba - by,

but you're still with ___ me in ___ my dreams. ___

And to - night, ___ there's on - ly you and me, ___

yeah. __

The ___ girl, there's on - ly you _ and me. _

__ Ev -'ry-thing _ I know   and ev -'ry -where _ I   go, __

it gets   hard, _____   but it _____ won't   take _

__ a - way __ my   love. _____

And when the last _ one falls,   when it's all ___ said and   done, _

it gets hard,____ but it____ won't take____

Gmaj7

____ a-way____ my love.____ Whoa,____ whoa.____

D.S. al Coda

D   A   Bm   G   A

CODA

G   A

____ girl, there's on - ly you__ and me,__

D   A   Bm

____ yeah,__ oh,__ yeah.____ Oh,__

G   A   Bm

oh,____ oh.____

HEY YA!

Words and Music by
ANDRE BENJAMIN

Moderately

One, two, three, uhh. My ba-by don't

mess a-round _ be-cause she loves me so _ and this I

know for shure, _____ uhh. But does she

real - ly want _ to but can't stand to see _ me walk _

out the door, _____ uhh? Don't try to

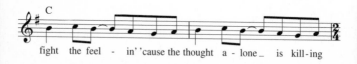

fight the feel - in' 'cause the thought a - lone _ is kill-ing

115

me right now, _____ uhh. Thank God for

mom and dad _ for stick ing two to-geth - er 'cause we

don't know how, _____ uhh. Hey _____

ya! _____ Hey ___ ya! _____

You think you've got it. Oh, ___ you think you've got it. But

got it just don't get it till there's noth - ing at all. _

_____ We get to-geth- er. Oh, _

— we get to geth - er. But sep'rate's al - ways bet - ter when there's

feel-ings in - volved. _____

If what they say is, "Noth - ing is for - ev - er," then

what makes, then what makes, then what makes, then

what makes, then what makes, huh, love the ex - cep - tion? _

— So why, oh? Why, oh? Why, _ oh? Why, oh? Why, oh are

we so in de - ni - al when we know we're not hap - py here? _____

Hey _____ ya! _____ Hey ___

Spoken: Y'all don't wanna hear me, you just wanna dance.

ya! _____ Don't want to meet your dad-dy, oh, oh. __

___ Just want you in my Cad-dy, oh, oh.

Oh, oh, ___ don't want to meet your ma-ma, oh, oh. __

___ Just want to make you cum-ma, oh, oh.

I'm, I'm, oh, oh, I'm just be-ing

hon-est. Oh, oh, ___ I'm just be-ing hon-est.

118

Rap 1: *(See additional lyrics)*

Play 4 times

Shake it.   Shake, shake it.   Shake it.   Shake, shake it.

Shake it.   Shake, shake it.   Shake it.   Shake it.   Shake, shake it.

Shake it   like   a   Po - la - roid   pic - ture.   Shake it.

Shake it.   Shake, shake it.   Shake it.   Shake, shake it.   Shake it.

Shake it.   Shake it, sug - ar.   Shake it   like   a   Po - la - roid

pic - ture. Shake it. Shake it. Shake, shake it.

Rap 2: *(See additional lyrics)*

Shake it. Shake, shake it. Shake it.

Shake it. Shake, shake it. Shake it like a Po - la - roid

G5 **C**

Hey _____ ya! _____

D **Em** **Repeat and Fade** **Optional Ending** **G5**

Hey _____ ya! _____

Additional Lyrics

          (3000): Hey, alright now. Alright now fellas!
Rap 1: (Fellas): Yeah!
          (3000): Now, what's cooler than being cool?
        (Fellas): Ice Cold!!!!
          (3000): Alright, alright, alright, alright, alright, alright, alright, alright.
                 Ok, now ladies.
        (Ladies): Yeah!!!!
          (3000): Now, we gon' break this thing down in just a few seconds.
                 Now, don't have me break this thing down for nothin'.
                 Now, I wanna see y'all on y'all baddest behavior.
                 Lend me some sugar, I am your neighbor, ahh. Here we go, uhh.

Rap 2: Now, all Beyonces and Lucy Lius and Baby Dolls get on the floor.
        You know what to do. You know what to do. You know what to do.

HOME

Words and Music by AMY FOSTER-GILLIES,
MICHAEL BUBLÉ and ALAN CHANG

Moderately slow

An - oth - er sum - mer day   has come and gone a - way

in Par - is and Rome, __ but I wan - na go home. __

May be sur - round - ed by   a mil - lion peo - ple; I

still feel all a - lone, __ just wan - na go home. __

__   Oh, I miss you, you know.   I've been

keep - ing all __ the let - ters __ that I wrote
feel just like __ I'm liv - ing __ some - one else -

to you,   each one   a   line ____
's   life.   It's like   I   just   stepped _

____ or two, __ "I'm fine,   ba - by, how are you?" _   I would
____ out-side __ when ev -'ry-thing was go-ing right. _   And I

send   them, but ___   I   know _   that   it's ___ just   not
know   just   why __   you   could _   not   come _   a - long

e - nough.   My   words   were   cold __
with   me: this ____   was   not __

____ and flat, ____   and you de-serve more _____ than that.
____ your dream, _ but you al-ways be - lieved _____ in   me.

An-oth-er ae - ro plane, an - oth - er sun-ny place; _
An-oth-er win-ter day has come and gone a-way ____

122

I'm luck - y, I know, but I wan - na go home, _
in ei - ther Par - is or Rome, and I wan - na go home, _

I've got to go home. Let me go home. _
let _ me go

I'm just too

far ____ from where you are; ____ I wan - na come

home. *Instrumental*

And I

home. _

And I'm sur - round - ed by a mil - lion peo - ple; I,

HOME

Words and Music by
CHRIS DAUGHTRY

Moderately

I'm star-in' out __ in-to __ the night __

try-ing to hide __ the pain.

I'm go-in' to __ the place __ where __ love __ and

feel-in' good __ don't ev-er cost __ a thing and the

pain you feel's __ a dif-f'rent kind __ of pain.

Well,
So, } I'm go-in' home, _____ back to the

Recorded a half step lower.

125

place where I____ be - long _____ and where your

love has al - ways been _ e - nough _ for me. ____

I'm not run - nin' from, _____ no, I

think you got __ me __ all __ wrong. I

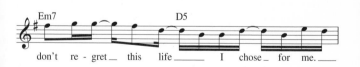

don't re - gret __ this life _____ I chose _ for me. ___

__ But these plac - es and _ these fac - es are get-ting ____

__ old, _____ so I'm go- in' home.

Well, I'm go - in' home.

The miles are get - ting long - er, ___ it seems, ___

the clos - er I get ___ to you. ___

I've not al - ways been ___ the best man ___ or friend ___

___ for you ___ but your love ___ re - mains ___ true ___

___ and I ___ don't ___ know ___ why. You

al - ways seem ___ to give ___ me an - oth - er ___

Csus2 **D.S. al Coda** **CODA** C5

_____ try. _

_____ old. _____

D

Be care - ful what _ you wish

C5

for _____ 'cause you just might get it all. _____

Em9 D5

_ You just might _ get it all _____

Csus2

_____ and then some you don't want. _

D

_____ Be care - ful what _ you wish

C5

for _____ 'cause you just might _ get it all. _____

You just might get it all, _____ yeah.

Oh ___

___ well, I'm go - in' home, ___ back to the

place where I___ be - long_____ and where your

love has al - ways been_ e - nough_ for me. ___

___ I'm not run - nin' from, ___ no, I

think you got___ me all_____ wrong. ___ I

HOW TO SAVE A LIFE

Words and Music by JOSEPH KING and ISAAC SLADE

Moderately

Step one, _ you say _ we need ____ to talk. He walks, _

_ you say, _ "Sit down, _ it's just _ a talk."

He smiles po - lite - ly back at you.

You stare po - lite - ly right on through

some sort of win - dow to ____ your right,

as he _ goes left ___ and you _ stay _ right.

IF IT MAKES YOU HAPPY

Words and Music by
JEFF TROTT and SHERYL CROW

Mar - i - lyn's sham - poo and Ben - ny Good - man's cor - set and pen.
mold off the bread, and serve you French toast a - gain.
played for mos - qui - toes, and ev - 'ry - where in be - tween.

Well, O K, I made this up. I
Well, O K, I still get stoned. I'm
Well, O K, we get a - long. So

prom - ised you I'd nev - er give up. If it makes you hap -
not the kind of girl you'd take home.
what if right now ev - ry - thing's wrong?

- py, it can't be that bad. If it makes you hap -

- py, then why the hell are you so sad?

You get down,

IF YOU'RE GONE

Written by ROB THOMAS

Moderately

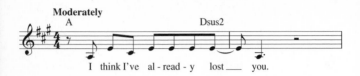

I think I've al-read-y lost ___ you.

I think you're al-read-y gone. ___

I think I'm fi-nal-ly scared _ now. You think I'm weak, _

___ I think you're wrong. ___

I think you're al-read-y leav - ing,

feels like your hand is on ___ the door. ___

JESUS TAKE THE WHEEL

Words and Music by BRETT JAMES,
GORDIE SAMPSON and HILLARY LINDSEY

Moderately slow

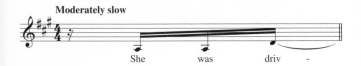

She   was   driv -

- ing last Friday on her way to Cin-cin-nat - i on a
lot on her mind, and she did-n't pay at-ten-tion.She was

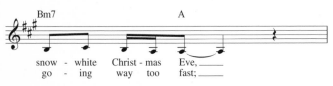

snow - white Christ - mas Eve,_____
go - ing way too fast;_____

go-ing home to see her mom - ma and her dad - dy with the
and be - fore __ she knew it, she was spin-ning on a

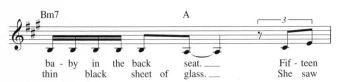

ba - by in the back seat. ____ Fif - teen
thin black sheet of glass. ____ She saw

miles to go, __ and she was run - ning _ low __ on
both their lives _ flash be - fore her __ eyes; _

faith and gas - o - line. ___ It'd been a

long hard __ year. ___ She had a

she did - n't e - ven have time to cry. ___ She was

so scared. _ She threw her hands up in __ the air: ___

"Je- sus, take _ the wheel; ___ take it from _ my hands, _

___ 'cause I can't do __ this on ____ my own. _

146

148

Vocal continues ad lib.

LIPS OF AN ANGEL

Words and Music by AUSTIN WINKLER,
ROSS HANSON, LLOYD GARVEY, MARK KING,
MICHAEL RODDEN and BRIAN HOWES

Slowly

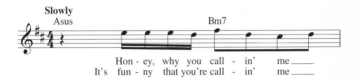

Hon - ey, why you call - in' me ____
It's fun - ny that you're call - in' me ____

so ____ late? ____
to - night; ____

It's kind-a hard to talk right ___ now. ___
and, yes, I've ___ dreamt of you, too. ___

Hon - ey, why you cry - in'? Is ev - 'ry -
It's just, I know you talk - in' ____ to me

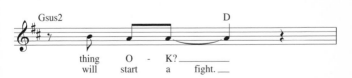

thing O - K? ____
will start a fight. ____

150

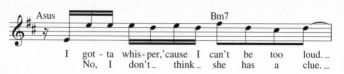

I got - ta whis - per,'cause I can't be too loud.
No, I don't think she has a clue.

Well, my girl's in the next room.

Some - times, I wish she was you.

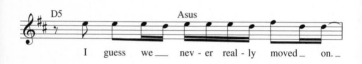

I guess we never real - ly moved on.

It's real - ly good to

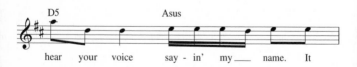

hear your voice say - in' my name. It

sounds so sweet. Com - in' from the

| D5 | Bb5 | C5 | D5 |

| Bb5 | C5 | A5 |

It's real-ly good to

| D5 | Asus |

hear your voice say-in' my __ name; it

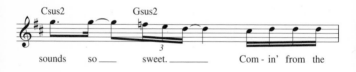

| Csus2 | Gsus2 |

sounds so __ sweet. _____ Com-in' from the

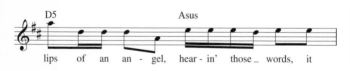

| D5 | Asus |

lips of an an-gel, hear-in' those_ words, it

| C5 | G5 |

makes me __ weak. _____ And __

| Bm7 |

I nev-er wan-na say__ good -

LISTEN TO YOUR HEART

Words and Music by PER GESSLE
and MATS PERSSON

Moderately, with feeling

I know there's some-thin' in the wake of your smile. _

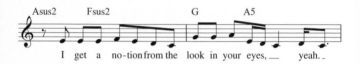

I get a no-tion from the look in your eyes, _ yeah. _

You've built a love _ but that love falls a - part. _ Your lit-tle piece of

heav-en turns to dark. _ Lis-ten to your

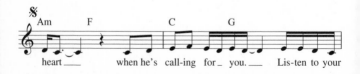

heart _ when he's call-ing for _ you. _ Lis-ten to your

156

lost in the tide, _ yeah. _ They're swept a - way _ and noth-ing

is what it seems. _ The feel-ing of be-long-ing _ to your dreams. _

D.S. al Coda

Lis-ten to your

CODA

you tell him _ good - bye. ____

Instrumental

And there are voic-es that

158

you tell him — good - bye. ——————

Lis-ten to your heart, ————— mm, mm. —

— I don't know where you're go - ing — and —

I don't know why — but lis-ten to your heart —— be - fore —

— you tell him — good -

bye. ——————

LOVE SONG

Words and Music by
SARA BAREILLES

Head un-der wa — ter, and they tell

— me to breathe eas - y for a while. —

The breath-ing gets hard - er; e-ven I —

— know — that. — Made room for me. —

It's too soon to see — if I'm hap-

- py in your — hands. — I'm un-u-su'l-ly —

160

CODA

all you have is leav - in', I'm gon - na

need a bet - ter rea - son to write ___ you a love ___

___ song to - day. ___ Prom - ise ___ me

that you'll leave the light on ___

to help me see ___ with day - light my

guide, gone. ___ 'Cause I be - lieve ___

___ there's a way ___ you can

164

MAKES ME WONDER

Words by ADAM LEVINE
Music by ADAM LEVINE, JESSE CARMICHAEL and MICKEY MADDEN

get be - hind; / - ter that, / make — your move. / af - ter that, / For - / try ——

get a - bout the truth. / — to get you back. / I still don't have the rea -

son and you don't have the time. — And it

real - ly makes me won-der if I ev - er gave a fuck a-bout

you. Give me some-thing to be - lieve in, 'cause I

don't be-lieve in you an - y - more, an - y - more. ——

I won-der if it e - ven makes a dif-f'rence to try. —

To Coda ⊕

Gmaj7   F#7

___ Oh no,   so this is good-bye.

Gmaj7   F#m7

And I've been here be-fore.   One day I'll wake up and it

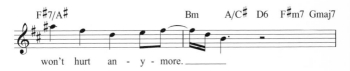

F#7/A#   Bm   A/C#   D6   F#m7 Gmaj7

won't hurt an - y - more. _____

F#m7

You caught me in a lie;   I have no al - i - bi.

F#7/A#   Bm

The words you say don't have a mean-ing, _ 'cause I

Gmaj9   A

still don't have _ the rea - son   and

Gmaj9   A   Bm   A

you don't have the time. _____   And it

100 YEARS

Words and Music by
JOHN ONDRASIK

Moderately fast

I'm fif - teen ___ for a mo - ment,

caught in ___ be - tween ___ ten and twen - ty and I'm

___ just dream - ing, ___ count - ing the ways ___

___ to where you are. ___

I'm twen - ty - two ___ for a mo - ment

172

Fif - teen, there's __ still time __ for you.

__ Time __ to buy __ and time _ to choose. _

__ Hey, fif - teen, there's nev - er a wish __

__ bet - ter than this __ when you

on - ly got __ a hun - dred years to live. _

__ *Instrumental*

A MOMENT LIKE THIS

Words and Music by JOHN REID
and JORGEN KJELL ELOFSSON

Moderately slow

What if I told you it was all meant to be?

Would you be-lieve me? Would you a-gree?

It's al-most that feel-ing we've met be-fore, so

tell me that you don't think I'm cra - zy when I

tell you love has come here and now.

Recorded a half step lower.

Ev-'ry-thing chang-es, but beau-ty re - mains __

some - thing so ten - der __ I can't ex - plain. _____

Well, I _____ may be dream - ing, but still lie a - wake. __

Can't we make __ this dream _ last _ for ev - er? __ And I'll

cher - ish all __ the love _____ we share. _

_____ A mo-ment like this. _____ Some peo ple wait _ a life-

- time for a mo - ment like this. __

Some peo-ple search _ for-ev - er for that one spe-cial kiss. _

_ Oh, I can't be - lieve _ it's hap -

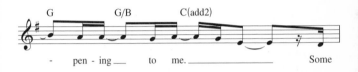

- pen - ing _ to me. _____ Some

peo-ple wait _ a life - time for a mo - ment like this. _

_ Could _ this be _ the great - est love _ of

all? I wan-na know that you _ will catch _ me when I fall, _

_____ so let me tell you this: _____ some

peo-ple wait _ a life - time for a mo-ment like this. _

— Some peo-ple wait _ a life - time for a mo-ment like this. _

___ Some peo-ple search _ for-ev - er for that one spe-cial kiss. _

___ Oh, I can't be - lieve _ it's hap -

- pen - ing ____ to me. _____ Some

183

people wait _ a life - time for a mo - ment _ like this. _

_____ *Choir:* (Mo-ment like this.) __
Lead vocal ad lib.

(Mo-ment like.) Oh, ___ I can't be-lieve __ it's hap-
Lead vocal:

- pen-ing _ to me. _____ Some peo-

- ple wait _ a life - time for a mo - ment _____ like _

this, oh, _____ like _ this. _____

ORDINARY PEOPLE

Words and Music by JOHN STEPHENS
and WILL ADAMS

Moderately fast

Girl, __ I'm in love with you, __

but this __ ain't the hon-ey-moon. __

We're past the in-fat-u-a-tion phase.

We're right __ in the thick of love. __

At times __ we get sick of love. __

It seems _ like we ar - gue ev - 'ry day. _

Fmaj13   B♭maj7

_ I know I've _ mis - be - haved _ and you've made _

E♭maj9

_ your mis - takes _ and we've both _

Fmaj9

_ still got room _ left to grow. _ And though love _

B♭maj7   E♭maj9

_ some-times hurts, _ I still _ put you first. _ And we'll make _

Fmaj9

_ this thing work, _ but I think _ we should take _ it slow. _

𝄋
B♭maj9   E♭maj9

_ We're _ just or - di-nar-y peo - ple. _

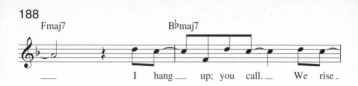

Fmaj7   B♭maj7

I hang __ up; you call. __ We rise __

E♭maj9

__ and we fall, ____ and we feel __

Fmaj9

__ like just walk - ing a - way. __ But as our __

B♭maj7   E♭maj9

__ love ad-vanc - es, we take __ sec-ond chanc - es. Though it's __

Fmaj9   **D.S. al Coda I**

__ not a fan - ta-sy, I ____ still want you __ to stay.

CODA I

Fmaj9

This time we'll take __ it slow. __ Take it slow. __

B♭m7

__ May - be we'll live and learn.

Db/Eb

May - be we'll crash and burn. __

Fmaj9

May - be you'll stay; may - be you'll

leave; may - be you'll __ re - turn. __

Bbm7

May - be an - oth - er fight; __

Db/Eb

may - be we won't sur - vive.

Fmaj9

But may - be we'll grow. We __ nev - er

D.S. al Coda II

know, ba - by, you __ and I. __

CODA II

REHAB

Words and Music by
AMY WINEHOUSE

Retro Blues

They tried to make me go to re - hab, I said,

"No, no, no." Yes,

I been black, but when I come back, you won't

know, know, know.

I ain't got the time, and if my

dad - dy ___ thinks ___ I'm fine, _____ he's

tried to make me go to re - hab, _ I ___ won't ___

go, _____ go, _____ go. _____

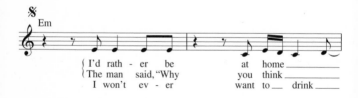

{ I'd rath - er be at home _____
{ The man said, "Why you think _____
I won't ev - er want to __ drink _____

___ with Ray, I ain't
___ you're here?" I said,
___ a - gain, I just,

got sev - en - ty days. _____ 'Cause there's
"I got no i - de - a, _____ I'm
ooh, I just need a _____ friend. _ I'm not

C7(no3)

shot   glass.   They
rest." _____   They   tried to make me go   to   re -

- hab, __ I __ said, __ "No, _____ no, _____ no." _

___   Yes, __ I been _ black, but when _

___ I come _ back, you won't know, ___ know, _ know. _

D.S. al Coda

CODA

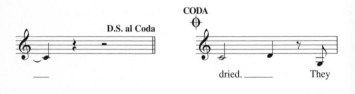

___   dried. _____   They

C7(no3)

tried to make me go   to re - hab, _ I __ said, _

STACY'S MOM

Words and Music by CHRIS COLLINGWOOD
and ADAM SCHLESINGER

Medium Rock

Sta-cy's mom _ has got _ it go-ing on.

Sta-cy's mom _ has got _ it go-ing on.

Sta-cy's mom _ has got _ it go-ing on.

Sta-cy's mom _ has got _ it go-ing on.

Sta-cy, can I come o - ver af-ter school? _
Sta-cy, do you re-mem - ber when I mowed your lawn? _

_____ (Af - ter school?) _
_____ (Mowed your lawn?) _

Sta-cy's mom _ has got _ it go-ing on. She's all I want _ and I've wait-ed for so _ long. _ Sta-cy, can't you see you're just not the girl _ for me? _ I know it might be wrong but I'm in love with Sta-cy's mom.

Instrumental

Sta-cy's mom _ has got _

SUGAR, WE'RE GOIN' DOWN

Words and Music by PATRICK STUMPH, PETER WENTZ,
ANDREW HURLEY and JOSEPH TROHMAN

Moderately slow

Am I more than you bar-gained for yet?
more than you bar-gained for yet?

I've been dy-in' to tell you
Oh, don't mind me, I'm watch-ing

an-y-thing you wan-na hear, __ 'cause
you two from the clos - et wish-ing to

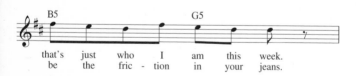

that's just who I am this week.
be the fric-tion in your jeans.

Lie in the grass __ next to the mau - so-le-
Is-n't it messed __ up, how I'm just dy-in' to be __

202

num - ber one___ with a bul - let,   a

load - ed god com - plex, cock it and pull it. We're go - in'

down,   down___ in an ear - li - er round,___ and

sug - ar, we're go - ing down swing - in'.   I'll be your

num - ber one___ with a bul - let,   a

load - ed god com - plex, cock it and pull it.

1
D/F♯   G5   A5   B5   C5   B5

2
Gsus2   E5   D5

Is   this

Down, down in an ear - li - er round, ___ and

sug - ar, we're go - ing down swing - in'. I'll be your

G5

num - ber one ___ with a bul - let, a

load - ed god com - plex, cock it and pull it. We're go - ing

D5

down, down ___ in an ear - li - er round, ___ and

sug - ar, we're go - ing down swing - in'. I'll be your

Gsus2

num - ber one ___ with a bul - let, a

N.C.

load - ed god com - plex, cock it and pull it. We're go - ing

A THOUSAND MILES

Words and Music by
VANESSA CARLTON

Moderately

Mak-ing my way down-town, walk - ing fast.

Fac - es pass and I'm home - bound.

Star-ing blank - ly a - head, just mak - ing my way,

mak - ing a way through the

crowd.

Recorded a half step higher.

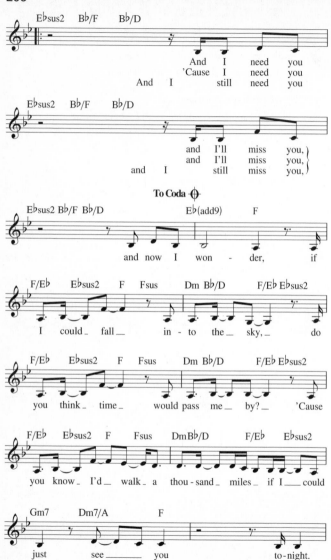

Instrumental (1.) It's
al - ways times _ like these _ when I think _ of you _
_ and I won - der if __ you ev - er
think of __ me. __ 'Cause
ev - 'ry - thing's _ so wrong _ and I don't _ be - long _
_ liv - ing in __ your pre - cious
mem - o - ry. __
Instrumental And

THIS LOVE

Words and Music by ADAM LEVINE and JESSE CARMICHAEL

___ a-gain, but oh. ___ oh. This love has tak-en its toll ___ on me. She said good-bye ___ too man-y times be-fore. And her heart is break-ing in front ___ of me. And I have no choice ___ 'cause I won't say good-bye an-y-more, ___ whoa, ___ whoa, ___ whoa. ___ I'll fix ___ these bro - ken things. ___

UMBRELLA

Words and Music by SHAWN CARTER, THADDIS L. HARRELL,
CHRISTOPHER STEWART and TERIUS NASH

Moderate Hip-Hop

Rap: *(See rap lyrics)* Eh, eh, eh.

Eh, eh, eh, eh.

Eh, eh, eh, eh, eh, eh, eh. You

had my heart __ and we'll nev - er be

worlds a - part. __ May - be in

mag - a - zines, _____ but you'll still

Recorded a half step lower.

Bm9
be my star. ___ Ba - by, 'cause

Gmaj7
in the dark ___ you can see

A
shin - y cars ___ and that's when you

F#m7   Bm9
need me there. _ With you I'll al - ways share be - cause _

G
___ when the sun shines, we'll shine to - geth -

D
er. Told you I'll be here for - ev -

A
er. Said I'll al - ways be your friend. _

Bm
___ Took an oath, I'm - a stick it out 'til the end. _

CODA

Bm9

eh,   eh,   eh,   eh,   eh.

C

You can run into my arms.

G

It's okay, don't be alarmed. Come

Dsus   D

in - to me, there's no dis - tance

A5 B5 C

in between our love. Gon-na let the rain

G   F#7

fall. I'll be all you need and more.

G

Be-cause, when the sun shines, we'll shine to-geth-

er. Told you I'll be here for-ev-

er. Said I'll al - ways be your friend. _

___ Took an oath, I'm - a stick it out 'til the end.

___ Now that it's rain - in' more than ev-

er, know that we'll still have each oth-

er. You can stand un - der my um - br-el -

la. You can stand un-der my um-br-el-la, el-la, el-la, eh,

eh, eh. Un-der my um-br-el - la, el - la, el - la, eh,

eh, eh. Un-der my um-br-el - la, el - la, el - la, eh,

eh, eh. Un-der my um-br-el - la, el - la, el - la, eh,

eh, eh, eh, eh, eh.   It's   rain-in', rain-in'.   Ooh, ba-by, it's

rain - in', rain - in'.   Ba - by, come in - to me, ___ come

in - to me. ___   It's   rain - in'. _____

Rap Lyrics

No clouds in my storms. Let it rain. I hydroplane into fame.
Comin' down with the Dow Jones. When the clouds come, we gone.
We Rockafella, she fly higher than weather and she rocks it better.
You know me. An anticipation for precipitation. Stack chips for the rainy day.
Jay, rain man is back wit' little Miss Sunshine. Rihanna, where you at?

WHITE FLAG

Words and Music by RICK NOWELS,
ROLLO ARMSTRONG and DIDO ARMSTRONG

Moderately slow

I know you think that I should-n't still love you, I'll
I know I left too much mess and de-struc-tion to come

tell you that. ___ But if
back a-gain. ___ And I caused

I did-n't say it, well, I'd still have felt it.
noth-ing but trou-ble; I un-der-stand if you can't

Where's the sense in that? ___ I prom-ise
talk to me a-gain. ___

I'm not try-ing to make your life hard-er; I'll re-turn ___
And if you live by the rules that it's o-ver, then I'm sure ___

___ to where we were. ___
___ that that makes sense. ___

222

UNDERNEATH IT ALL

Words and Music by DAVID A. STEWART and GWEN STEFANI

Moderate Reggae

It's times when I want some - one more, ___

__ a - some-one more like me,

and there's times when this __ dress re - hears - al

seems in - com - plete, _____ but

you see the col - ors in __ me like __
you give me the __ most gor - geous sleep __

__ that I've ev - er had, _____
__ no one else _____

226

but late - ly you've been try - ing real __ hard and

giv - ing me __ your best, _____ and

love - ly. _____

It's so man - y moons that we __ have seen __

___ a - stum - bl - ing back next __ to me. __

I've seen right through and un - der - neath, __

___ and you make __ me bet - ter. ___

I've seen right through and un - der - neath, __

and you make me bet - ter,

bet - ter bet - ter. For real, 'cause un-der-

neath it all, you are my real Prince Charm - ing. Like the

heat from the fi - re you were al - ways burn - ing. An - y -

time you're a-round my bod - y keeps call - ing for your

touch, your kiss-es and your sweet ro - manc - ing. There's an -

oth - er side of you a - dis a-wom-an here a - dore. A -

side from your tem - per ev -'ry-thing else se - cure. You -'re

WE BELONG TOGETHER

Words and Music by MARIAH CAREY, JERMAINE DUPRI,
MANUEL SEAL, JOHNTA AUSTIN, DARNELL BRISTOL,
KENNETH EDMONDS, SIDNEY JOHNSON, PATRICK MOTEN,
BOBBY WOMACK and SANDRA SULLY

Slow Soul

I did-n't mean it when I said I did-n't love you so.

I should have held on tight, I nev-er should-'ve let you go.

I did-n't know noth-ing. I was stu-pid. I was fool-ish. I was

lyin' to my - self.

I could not fath-om that I would ev - er be with-out your love.

fig - ure out where the hell I went

wrong. The pain re - flect - ed in this

song ain't e - ven half of what I'm

feel-ing in - side. _ I need you, need you back in my life. _

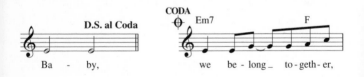

Ba - by, we be - long _ to - geth - er,

ba - by. _ When you left I lost a part of

me. _ It's still so hard to be - lieve. _ Come back,

ba - by, please, __ 'cause we be - long __ to - geth -

er. Who am I gon - na lean on when times get

rough? Who's gon-na talk to me till the sun comes

up? Who's gon-na take your place? __ There ain't no - bod - y bet -

- ter. Oh, ba - by, ba - by, we be - long __ to - geth -

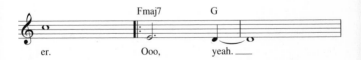

er. Ooo, yeah. __

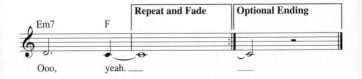

Repeat and Fade   **Optional Ending**

Ooo, yeah. __   __

WHAT HURTS THE MOST

Words and Music by STEVE ROBSON and JEFFREY STEELE

Moderately slow

I can take the rain on the roof of this
It's hard to deal _ with the pain of los - in' you ev - 'ry -

emp - ty house, ___ that don't both - er me.
where I go, ___ but I'm do - in' it.

I can take a few tears now and then and just
It's hard to force _ that smile when I see our old

let 'em out. ___ I'm not a -
friends and I'm a - lone. Still hard - er

fraid to cry, ev - 'ry once in a while e - ven though
get - tin' up, get - tin' dressed, liv - in' with this re - gret,

go - in' on   with you gone   still   up - sets   me.
but   I know   if   I could   do   it   o - ver,

There are   days   ev - 'ry now   and a - gain   I pre-tend
I would trade, give a - way   all the words that   I saved

I'm   O - K,   but   that's   not   what   gets   me.
in   my   heart,   that   I   had   nev - er   spo - ken.

What   hurts   the most   was be - in'

so ____ close   and hav - in' so   much to say

and watch - in' you   walk a - way. ____

238

YOU ARE THE MUSIC IN ME

from the Disney Channel Original Movie
HIGH SCHOOL MUSICAL 2

Words and Music by
JAMIE HOUSTON

Moderately fast Rock

Na, na, na, na, __ na, na, na, na, __ yeah.

__ You are the mu-sic in me.

You know, the words, __ "once up-on a time" make you lis-

- ten. There's a rea - son. When you dream, __ there's a

chance you'll find _____ a lit-tle laugh-ter or "hap-py

ev - er af - ter." You're a har - mo - ny _____ to the

mel - o - dy_____ that's ech - o - ing_ in - side_

_ my head._ A sin - gle voice_ a -

bove the noise, _ and like a com-mon thread,

mmm, you're pull - ing me. When I hear my fa -

v'rite song, I know that we be - long. Oh, _ you_

_ are the mu - sic in me. Yeah, it's liv - ing in all

of us, and it's brought us here _ be - cause_

Bb(add2) — C
you are the mu-sic in me.__ Na, na, na, na,

Bb6 — F
na, na, na, na, na, na, na, na, na.

Bb — F(add2)
You are the mu-sic in me.____ It's like I knew you be-fore

C — Bb
we met. Can't ex-plain,__ there's no name__

F
__ for__ it. I sang you words__ I've nev-

C — Bb
er said, and it__ was eas-y, be-cause you

F — C/E — Dm
see the real__ me. As I am__ you un-

Bb(add2) ... **Dm7**

_____ are the mu - sic in me. (Me.) _____

C/E

_____ To - geth - er we're gon - na sing. (Sing.) _____

Bbmaj9

_____ We got the pow - er to say ___ what we feel, ___ con -

nect - ed and real, ___ can't keep it all ___ in - side. ___

C ... **Bb6**

_____ Na, na, na, na. Na, na, na, na, na.

F ... **Bb**

Na, na, na, na. You ___ are the mu - sic in me. ___

C ... **Bb6**

_____ Na, na, na, na. Na, na, na, na, na.

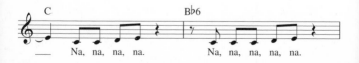

Na, na, na, na. You __ are the mu - sic in me. __

__ When I hear my fa - v'rite song, I know that we

be - long. You __ are the mu - sic in me. __

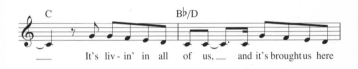

__ It's liv - in' in all of us, __ and it's brought us here

be - cause you __ are the mu - sic in me.

Na, na, na, na. Na, na, na, na, na. Na, na, na, na. You __

__ are the mu - sic in me. __

YOU RAISE ME UP

Words and Music by BRENDAN GRAHAM
and ROLF LOVLAND

YOU'RE BEAUTIFUL

Words and Music by JAMES BLUNT,
SACHA SCARBECK and AMANDA GHOST

Moderately slow

My life is bril - liant,

my love is pure.

I saw an an - gel,

of that I'm sure. She smiled

at me on the sub - way, she was

with an - oth - er man. But I

GUITAR CHORD FRAMES

	C	Cm	C+	C6	Cm6
C					

	C♯	C♯m	C♯+	C♯6	C♯m6
C♯/D♭					

	D	Dm	D+	D6	Dm6
D					

	E♭	E♭m	E♭+	E♭6	E♭m6
E♭/D♯					

	E	Em	E+	E6	Em6
E					

	F	Fm	F+	F6	Fm6
F					

This guitar chord reference includes 120 commonly used chords. For a more complete guide to guitar chords, see "THE PAPERBACK CHORD BOOK" (HL00702009).

	C7	Cmaj7	Cm7	C7sus	Cdim7
C					

	C♯7	C♯maj7	C♯m7	C♯7sus	C♯dim7
C♯/D♭					

	D7	Dmaj7	Dm7	D7sus	Ddim7
D					

	E♭7	E♭maj7	E♭m7	E♭7sus	E♭dim7
E♭/D♯					

	E7	Emaj7	Em7	E7sus	Edim7
E					

	F7	Fmaj7	Fm7	F7sus	Fdim7
F					

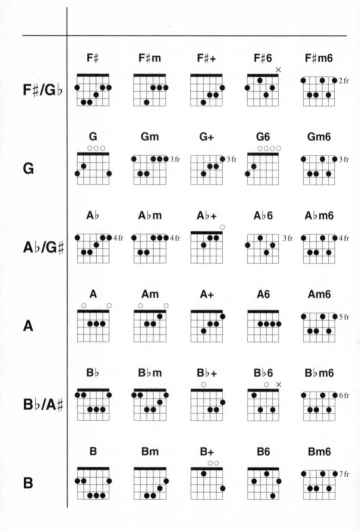

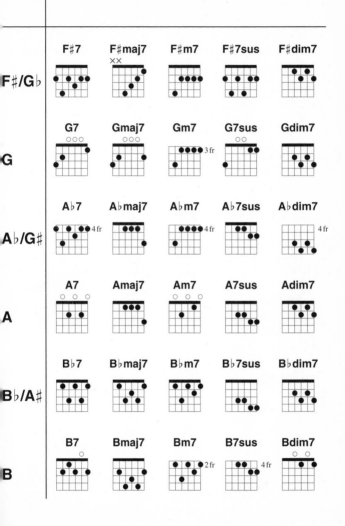

PAPERBACK SONGS

THE '20S
00240236

THE '30S
00240238

THE '40S
00240239

THE '50S
00240240

THE '60S
00240241

THE '70S
00240242

THE '80S
00240243

THE '90S
00240244

'80S & '90S ROCK
00240126

THE BEATLES
00702008

BIG BAND SWING
00240171

THE BLUES
00702014

BROADWAY SONGS
00240157

CHILDREN'S SONGS
00240149

CHORDS FOR KEYBOARD & GUITAR
00702009

CHRISTMAS CAROLS
00240142

CHRISTMAS SONGS
00240208

CLASSIC ROCK
00310058

CLASSICAL THEMES
00240160

COUNTRY HITS
00702013

NEIL DIAMOND
00702012

GOOD OL' SONGS
00240159

GOSPEL SONGS
00240143

HYMNS
00240103

INTERNATIONAL FOLKSONGS
00240104

JAZZ STANDARDS
00240114

LATIN SONGS
00240156

LOVE SONGS
00240150

MOTOWN HITS
00240125

MOVIE MUSIC
00240113

POP/ROCK
00240179

ELVIS PRESLEY
00240102

THE ROCK & ROLL COLLECTION
00702020

RODGERS & HAMMERSTEIN
00240177

SOUL HITS
00240178

TV THEMES
00240170

FOR MORE INFORMATION, SEE YOUR LOCAL MUSIC DEALER,
OR WRITE TO:

HAL•LEONARD®
CORPORATION
7777 W. BLUEMOUND RD. P.O. BOX 13819 MILWAUKEE, WI 53213

www.halleonard.com